Reflections On The Path: The Awakening

Linda M. Robinson

Acknowledgements

I am fortunate to have had the support and encouragement from many persons along my path, and for this, I am truly grateful…

To Ronna Herman and James Tyberonn and Anne for their mentorship and guidance and for introducing me to realms beyond my imagination.

To Lou for mentorship and guidance in all areas of spirituality.

To Cathy and Arielle for their encouragement and support throughout this process.

To my friends for their encouragement and support all along my path.

To my brother George for his unwavering support, acceptance, and friendship.

To Lynne for developing my website.

To Angela Gaye, Merri, Angela, Cheryl, Moyra, and Frank for assistance with helping me take this book from its raw form and transforming it into a finished product.

To my guides and teachers in the Higher Realms who made this journey possible and encouraged me to soar with the angels.

Contents

Prologue

You cannot step into the same river twice, for the water into which you first stepped has flowed on. – Heraclitus

Life is a series of stepping-stones. One step leads to the next. Often it is not until you look back that you realize each stone represents a choice that was setting the direction for the next step and adventure.

When you look at the steps from a higher perspective, you can see a pattern and how a beautifully orchestrated path has unfolded. When you follow your heart and take each step as it appears, magic seemingly occurs. In reality, the magic results from following an inner prompting to take a course of action.

With any path, following your heart takes courage. It often requires you to step outside your comfort zone of the familiar in order to embrace the new and unknown. Sometimes you are forever changed by this process.

This book shows how my path has magically unfolded as I became open to the possibilities. It is a path that went from a very conservative, traditional background to one of awakening and embracing spirituality and metaphysics.

It is a path of finding my voice and having the courage to speak about what I have learned. Each stepping stone on the path can be considered as a vignette, a tool, or a realization that contributed to my growth.

As I moved along my path, I encountered many new ideas and

concepts. I immediately resonated with some, others I discarded because they didn't feel right for me, and I wasn't sure about a few.

I set aside the ones I wasn't sure about for later consideration. As you read this book and learn about the stepping-stones on my path and the concepts I encountered, I invite you to use the same approach. Your heart will tell you what is right for you.

It is in the looking back that I can see the lessons I have learned and how my choices have defined my journey. I can see how the smallest actions can develop into major changes on one's path.

As I share with you the steps of my journey, I am also sharing the wisdom I have gained from each step. It is this wisdom and how we apply it to our next step that determines which direction we will take when we reach the fork in the road.

I invite you to join me on my journey.

Part 1

~~~

My Awakening

The Beginning of the Dawn

The sun peeked over the horizon and burst into a glorious orb of light. As I awoke to this magnificent sight, the day was full of promise. It would turn out to be a very auspicious day and one that would change my life forever.

It was May 1978, and I had just completed ten weeks of training to work as a volunteer for a crisis hotline. During that time, I had formed many friendships with the other members of my training group. Tonight we planned to celebrate with a festive dinner and shared remembrances of our training.

As the day turned to dusk, we gathered at the home of one of the members. We enjoyed a delicious potluck meal, and then the conversation turned to the mutual interests of several of the members.

One member mentioned that she did energy work. This was a completely foreign term to me. She suggested to another member that they do a demonstration of what the energy could do. As one member lay on the floor, another member passed her hands over his body from head to feet. This continued for several minutes.

At the end of this exercise, the person on the floor commented that he was in an altered space. I didn't know what that meant and didn't ask. I didn't want to show my ignorance. How could passing the hands over the body from head to feet produce an altered state? And what was an altered state?

The person on the floor then yielded his position to someone else. Each person was smiling and happy after getting up from the floor. But why?

This continued until it was my turn. I panicked because this was completely new to me! Although I trusted the person performing the energy exercise, I didn't trust myself. What if I lost control? What might I do?

So I politely declined the offer. Still, my curiosity was heightened by what I had witnessed.

Sensing my interest, someone mentioned that I might want to check out Edgar Cayce's A.R.E., the Association for Research and Enlightenment, in Virginia Beach. I learned that it is an organization founded by Edgar Cayce to focus on the information in his readings and the topics that frequently came up in them.

Several days later one of my new friends called and offered to go with me to the A.R.E. so that I could see what was available. There I learned that Edgar Cayce, who lived from 1877-1945, was a famous psychic who did readings for people on topics that included health, past lives, and other spiritual topics.

As I focused on this, I felt excited. I had discovered a world that was previously unknown to me. Little did I know that the trip to the A.R.E. and my discovery of metaphysics would change my life forever!

How Could This Be?

Nothing in my background had prepared me for my new adventures into the world of metaphysics and spirituality.

As a young child in the rural South of the United States, I had a good, secure childhood growing up on a farm. My family consisted of my father and mother and a brother who was four years younger than I was.

An extended family of aunts and uncles visited often or we visited them, and I spent many wonderful hours with them. For the first four years of my life, my paternal grandmother and aunt lived with us, and I was very fortunate to have extra attention from them. In my playtime, I loved walking in the woods, and I felt very much at peace among the trees.

Lifestyles were very traditional, and conforming to social norms was important. One area in which this was evident was in the role of women. Women were expected to take a secondary role to men.

Even as a young child, I couldn't understand this. Why weren't women considered to be equal to men? Something seemed out-of-balance in the diminution of women. I knew that women were just as smart and capable as men, so why weren't they considered equal?

I had known from a very early age that my path would not be a traditional one. I had somehow known that I would not have children and that I would have a career outside the home. This was quite a departure from the societal expectations for a young girl in the rural South!

Education was very important. It was considered to be the ticket to a better life, and from an early age, I knew that I would be going to college. My mother and several of my aunts and uncles had college degrees, so the importance of continuing my education was instilled in me throughout my childhood. I daydreamed about what it would be like and where I would decide to go.

Pleasing others was also very important. You were expected to put others first, even if it would be detrimental to your own well being. You were taught to hide your feelings and not to let others know how you were feeling or what you wanted to do. So, being a dutiful

Southern girl, I complied with this norm.

The accepted measuring stick for making decisions was, "What will the neighbors think?" If an action might prompt an unfavorable reaction from others, then that action had to be scrapped. Being highly thought of was very important. Nothing could be done that would deviate from the customs of the area.

Traditional religion was the order of the day. My family was very active in the Methodist church in our community. Everyone was expected to go to Sunday School and church every Sunday. There were no exceptions unless one was sick or on vacation. You were expected to believe what you were taught in church and not to question the accepted interpretations of the Bible. Again, I complied with the expectations.

I had always wondered about the rest of life that didn't fit into what I learned in church. What about people of other beliefs? Were there also periods of history that weren't covered in what I was taught?

There always seemed to be a missing piece, but I didn't know enough to ask questions. I just went along with the traditional life and beliefs. Yet, somehow, I always felt that there was something more. I had a deep inner yearning in the core of my Being for something that seemed to be missing.

So… imagine my surprise and excitement when I first entered the doors of the A.R.E. and went into the bookstore. There were books on topics I had never encountered -- reincarnation, other lives, other beliefs, and expanded views of spirituality.

How could I have lived just forty-five minutes from this oasis for eight years without discovering what was in my backyard? I was like a child in a candy store!

The friend who accompanied me suggested that I might like to read *There Is A River* by Thomas Sugrue, which is a biography of Edgar Cayce.

Then I noticed another book on other lives – past lives. Something stirred within me, and I had a feeling of returning home.

I purchased both books and could hardly wait to read them. I discovered upon reading Cayce's biography that he, too, had grown up in the church and had continued to read the Bible throughout his life. He had bridged the world of traditional religion with that of the paranormal and metaphysics. I felt encouraged.

Then I delved into the book on reincarnation. That was when I knew I had found the missing link that had plagued me for so long. Pieces began to fall into place. I could see how other beliefs all led to the same place of the One Creator.

From that point on, I was hooked. I read and read and read. The more I read, the more I wanted to know.

After I had read and studied everything I could get my hands on, I realized that my intense desire for that "something more" had sent powerful vibrations out into the ethers, and the Universe had arranged for me to take the volunteer training and to be placed in a training group with those who were interested in metaphysics.

As I look back on this, I can see that this is an example of "Be careful what you ask for. You may get it." In this case, it yielded the results for which I had asked.

It was a perfect illustration of the Universal Law of Attraction. Like attracts like.

In the Law of Attraction, your thoughts and emotions are very powerful and send out signals to the Universe. They attract things of a similar vibration. Like attracts like. Monitoring your thoughts and emotions can help you attract what you desire and avoid what you do not wish to have.

Don't Shout From the Rooftops Yet

My new enthusiasm for metaphysics brought an excitement to my life for which I had been yearning. I wanted to shout from the rooftops about my new discovery. However, I could not do it at that time. It was not yet possible.

After I had graduated from high school, I went to college in my home state of North Carolina and graduated early. I got married and moved to the Hampton Roads area of Virginia.

I was working as a teacher of life skills for adults and youth for an agency with traditional values, and I did not want to jeopardize my job, which I loved. This was the career I had dreamed about as a child.

I was married and had a very comfortable lifestyle.

Once again, the old measuring stick of "What will people think?" had re-surfaced. Instead of shouting from the rooftops about my new discovery, I could only share my excitement with a few like-minded friends. So, I continued to read and read and read.

Following the Signs on the Path

As I continued to read, I could look back on my life and see how everything had unfolded up to that moment to put me on this metaphysical path. After I had been working for a few years, my supervisor told me that if I wanted to progress in my career, I needed to continue my formal studies and complete a Master's Degree.

I had recently felt that there was something more I was supposed to be doing with my life, so I thought, "Maybe going back to graduate school is it."

I knew that there was a Master of Education in Guidance and

Counseling program at a nearby college. It was within driving distance for me, which meant that I could go to school at night while I continued to work full-time during the day.

The bonus was the choice of a major in counseling. I had always been interested in what people did, their personalities, and how their life paths evolved. This was a perfect fit for me.

As I approached the completion of my degree, I asked my university advisor how I might get more counseling experience. He suggested volunteering at a local crisis hotline.

I called the agency, and I was in luck. A training program for new volunteers was beginning the next month! I went for an interview, I was accepted as a hotline trainee, and I was on my way!

Part 2

~~~

Many New Concepts

Reincarnation?

One of the concepts in my reading that fascinated me most was reincarnation. As I mentioned earlier, this seemed to be the missing link in what I had been taught in my traditional church where there was no mention of reincarnation.

The religion I grew up in was a story of one lifetime where you would either go to Heaven or Hell and your one chance was contained in that one lifetime. There were no second chances if you got it wrong.

Your lot in life was determined in great part by where fate determined you were born. If you were born into a situation with many advantages, it was considered to be "by the grace of God." There was no explanation for why some were born into these situations and others were not. How could there be a God who gave special favors to some and not to others?

When I began to read about reincarnation, I started looking at lifetimes through a different lens. I began to learn how each incarnation is selected for the lessons that the Soul needs to experience to enable it to progress. Intentions, choices, and actions in one life can determine what course an individual lifetime will take as well as what lifetime is selected for the next incarnation.

Slowly, I began to realize that there was a pattern to what occurs. There was indeed a reason for each lifetime. It was not a reward or punishment, nor was it given "by the grace of God." It was rather an opportunity for the Soul to learn and grow and advance.

The degree to which we master the lessons we came to learn in one lifetime can influence our next incarnation. This is not as a reward or punishment but rather for the advancement of the Soul.

Each incarnation is selected by the Soul and its group of advisors in the Higher Realms after a review of the lifetime just completed. The location, gender, family, and other factors are considered for the advancement of the Soul in its next lifetime. Many times a Soul reincarnates with others who have shared previous lifetimes.

Had I Lived Before?

As I continued to read, I wondered, "Have I lived before? If so, who was I? When and where did I live? What did I do?" So many questions! And, how would I find the answers?

As I had learned previously when I discovered metaphysics, when an individual is ready, a teacher appears. Again, it was a case of a request I had sent forth to the Universe. My intense desire had sent forth a vibration that put me in direct contact with one avenue for my answer.

I saw an ad in the newspaper for a seminar on dreams. I had always had dreams, but I never considered them of much importance. Then I thought, "Why not? This sounds interesting. I think I'll go."

I was fascinated as I listened to the speaker discuss how dreams can give us guidance as well as answers to our questions. Close to the end of the presentation, she also mentioned that dreams may give us clues to past lives. My ears perked up. This is why I was guided to this class.

I bought her book and learned much more about how we can get clues to past lives from our dreams. I began recording my dreams and found the symbolism to be fascinating.

Then one night, I hit pay dirt in the dream world.

The Monastery – Life as a Monk

I saw myself on a tropical island during the 1500s. It was a beautiful setting with lush greenery and beautiful blue ocean waves lapping the shores.

I looked at the scene and realized I was a monk – a male in that lifetime. I was strolling along the banks of the island with another monk. A small stone cross was at the rear of the monastery.

Nothing in the dream stood out to me, and I had no strong emotions attached to it. So, I recorded the dream and didn't give it another thought until a year later.

I was scheduled to take a vacation on the island of Barbados. I had been looking forward to the trip, as I needed a respite from my busy work schedule.

When I arrived in Barbados, the land felt familiar. It seemed very comfortable. I felt as if I had returned home.

One day I took a guided tour of the island. It was to include several tourist sites, including a church. Still, I had no expectations beyond a pleasant day of sightseeing.

However, when the tour van rounded the corner and began the drive up a gentle hill, I saw a familiar site. It was the monastery of my dream! My heart almost jumped out of my body! I could hardly believe what I was seeing!

I immediately recognized the church as my former monastery home. Although the foliage had grown larger in present-day conditions, there was no mistake that it was the same location I had seen in my dream.

I jumped out of the van and walked around to the rear of the church. I saw the same familiar stone cross, and I knew that this had been my former home.

All too soon, it was time to leave the church and continue on the tour. However, this was my proof that I had, indeed, lived before. It was a remembrance beyond the shadow of a doubt.

The Law of One

A year later I went on a vacation to the island of St. Maarten in the Caribbean. It was a wonderful time of relaxation and touring. I had purchased several metaphysical books to read while I lounged on the beach. I was reading the story of one man's spiritual journey, and suddenly I came across a passage where he was discussing Atlantis and mentioned the Law of One.

Something stirred in my Soul. It resonated to the core of my Being. I knew without a doubt that I had lived in Atlantis and had been a part of the Law of One, the group who adhered to the laws of the Creator.

After I returned from that vacation, I was sitting in the meditation room of the A.R.E. As I gazed out onto the balcony of concrete and pebbles, I found myself walking along the beach in ancient Greece, in a place that had been part of Atlantis.

In my vision of that lifetime, I was wearing a flowing white robe that fastened on one shoulder. I had rope sandals on my feet. As I gazed out across the horizon in my vision, I knew that as a priestess in the Law of One during the time of Atlantis, I had had a great responsibility to help guide the people of my land. A time of decision for the continent would soon arrive.

Bathed in the Light

The feeling I had from realizing that I had been part of the Law of One stayed with me.

Then one day as I was driving to a meeting, I passed through a beautiful green area along the interstate highway. Suddenly, at a 45-degree angle off to the left above my third eye, an area of white light appeared.

As I focused on it and basked under it, it beamed down on me. I felt **total** love and peace. I wanted to go with it, but I knew I had to continue on to my meeting. For a few minutes I basked in the total love of the white light. Then it disappeared.

The events of the rest of the day seemed insignificant after the experience of the Light.

I was transformed by the Light. The feelings I had in that moment were the most profound I had ever felt, and the experience transcended any previous occurrence.

Many things became clear. I wanted to read all of my metaphysical books in five minutes, and yet I felt that I had read them already. I still believed in reincarnation, but it didn't matter. Nothing mattered except the love I had felt from the Light.

Then I realized that, ultimately, nothing matters except total love.

An Unexpected Message

Many times the Universe will give us messages about our path in unexpected ways. One such occurrence happened when I went for a routine dental check-up with my dentist, who followed a very traditional religious path.

Imagine my surprise when he came into the room and said, "I have a message for you. May I share it with you?" I immediately said, "Yes," anxious to hear what he had to tell me.

He said, "You have a great mission ahead of you. I'm not sure what it is, but I felt very strongly I had to share this with you." Then he said a brief prayer for me.

The night before my appointment I had felt that I was at a fork in the road and had a choice to make.

Reiki

Sometimes when there is something we are supposed to experience, it will reappear several times. This was the case for me with energy work.

Many times after I had passed up the opportunity to feel the energy at the group celebration after my crisis hotline training, I had wondered what I had missed. What if I had experienced the energy then? How would I have felt? How would I have responded?

The Universe heard my call and arranged for me to hear about a Reiki Level I class that was coming up. I thought, "Why not? This is my chance to see what energy is all about." So, I enrolled for the weekend class, and away I went.

I learned that the word Reiki means Universal Life Force. It consists of the energy practitioner attuning to the higher energy and allowing it to flow through them to the recipient. Although there is a set of hand positions for the practitioner, the energy usually flows to the area that the client needs.

I found that I really enjoyed the process, both as the practitioner and the recipient. And I didn't lose control of myself in the process, as I had been so afraid of years earlier. One more hurdle crossed!

At the end of the weekend I felt as if I had been on vacation for a week! Time had shifted to give me the peaceful interlude I needed.

Readings and Channeling

Another huge event happened when someone asked if I had ever had a reading. A reading…I had heard about the readings done by Edgar Cayce, but what was this? Was this the same, or was it different?

How could it apply to me? This stretched my mind even more.

I learned that some persons can do psychic readings by a number of methods – cards, psychometry or holding an object belonging to the person getting the reading, or any number of methods. Usually, the reader or channel tunes into the recipient's energy and receives impressions or information. Sometimes the reader's guides or the recipient's guides will bring information.

Some readers even go into a trance state during which they allow the guides to take control of their body. However, many readers are conscious channels. Their own consciousness steps to the side while the information is being given by a guide, but they are always aware and listening.

I had always been fascinated by tarot cards without knowing why, so I just happened, or rather the Universe arranged for me, to be put in contact with someone who did readings using tarot cards. I arrived with some trepidation for my reading. Was this real, or was it just fortune telling? What if I heard something that would upset me?

The psychic had me mix the cards up through a gentle shuffling and then select and lay out a certain number of cards. She proceeded to tell me what she "saw" for me in relationships, career, finance, and other areas.

She later explained that she was giving me what she saw at the moment and that I could change the direction of events based on my thoughts, intentions, and actions. If it happened to be an event over which I had little control, I could at least be mentally prepared and control my reactions to it. I felt okay about what I had received after she explained what a reading really was.

Then I met someone who did psychic readings by tuning into the person's vibrations and their guides and teachers. I was instructed to write down a list of questions on a piece of paper, fold it up, and bring it with me to the reading.

After saying a prayer, the medium took the folded paper in her hands and began to bring through my guides and teachers. They answered every question on the paper even though it still remained folded. When the medium told me to look at the paper and see if everything had been covered, I was astounded to see that it was.

Then she mentioned that she would be teaching a four-week introductory channeling class if I wanted to learn more. Did I ever! I promptly signed up for what, until that time, had always remained a mystery to me. She explained that it would be helpful for me to meditate ahead of time and to arrive ready to work.

My Channeling Begins

At the first session, she explained that during the four-week class, we would become acquainted with several of our guides and teachers. Each week would build on the previous one.

I watched as each person sat in the special chair that she used. It was surrounded with her good energy, and this helped to attune each of us to a higher energy. She also placed her hands on top of our head just before we began to channel.

It was a new process for me, and I was very apprehensive. Would I be able to channel? How would I know it was a Higher Being and not just myself? She said to relax and see what came through.

Melody

Soon it was my turn to sit in the special chair. As she placed her hands on my head and said a prayer, I felt a higher level of energy come in – an energy with a higher vibration.

Imagine my amazement when I heard a voice come out of my mouth and say, "Hello. This is Melody." This is all that came through on my first attempt.

I later learned that Beings in the Spirit World must lower their vibration at the same time we raise ours to be able to speak. Then I understood why it was so important for me to do my part to keep my own vibration as high as possible.

Melody came through in another session and told me that she was my gatekeeper and joy guide. She said she would assist me in the beginning with my channeling as well as bringing me joy. She said that, as my gatekeeper, she would only allow other Beings who had a positive, higher, compatible vibration to speak through me.

It was no coincidence that her name was Melody because at that time, songs would often pop into my head when I was in the shower. The guides were using the conductivity of water to open my receptivity. Usually when I focused on the words of the song, I could see that it was not a random occurrence but that the song had a specific message for me.

My guides were doing what any teacher does – start with the student wherever she is. This builds the student's comfort level and confidence and gives her something to which she can relate.

In my case, they brought me songs that I enjoyed so that I would focus on the words.

Some of the early songs they brought were Christian hymns because the words were very familiar. "Under the Guidance of Angels" was a favorite, and they brought this to let me know they were watching over me and working with me.

In later years they would bring me funeral music, to alert me to an impending disaster or someone making their transition to spirit. One such occurrence happened just hours before the space shuttle, Challenger, accident.

I was shopping for office supplies when the Marine hymn began playing in my head. Imagine my shock when I returned home and turned on the television to learn that the Challenger had exploded.

It has taken me some time to adjust to receiving this type of message. When it comes, I feel a sense of dread because I don't know what it means. However, I have come to appreciate the warning so that I have some forewarning. Now, when I get this music, I know that I am being prepared or alerted for what is to come.

Tall Oak

Another guide who came in to me during the channeling class was a Native American named Tall Oak. He said he was there to protect me.

Again, he selected a name that resonated with me, since we had many oak trees at the farm where I grew up. Every time he came through or I thought about him, I felt very protected because I knew he was there, watching over me. I didn't realize how much I would soon need his protection.

Confucius

The last session of the channeling class was devoted to the Ascended Masters and other Higher Beings. The teacher explained that the Ascended Masters would bring through high level information and wisdom teachings.

Would I be able to do this?

It was as if my teacher had read my thoughts.

She said, "Everyone will be able to bring through a Higher Being. You have all prepared for this, and your intent is there for bringing through the highest and the best."

When it was my turn to sit in the special chair, I took my place, and the teacher placed her hands on my head. I felt some very high energy come in.

Soon, I heard a voice speak through me:

This is Confucius. I bring you greetings.

My body was still adjusting to bringing through a Being of such high energy, so his message was very brief, but I was elated.

I knew that I wanted to meditate and practice more with my channeling so that I could bring through messages from the Ascended Masters and other Higher Beings of Light. That made my heart sing!

Quiet Time and Internal Growth

I had a period of intense growth, learning, and development in the mid-1980s. This was when I began to channel, and I met several persons who would become my teachers and mentors.

It was no accident that the Universe arranged for this time of intense growth to coincide with the Harmonic Convergence on August 16, 1987. For me, this occurrence felt like another gateway had opened.

I marked the day by attending an event coordinated by some of my teachers and like-minded individuals. I also spent much of the day thinking about what the Universe had in store for me next.

I can look back now and see that this was indeed a time of preparation for what was to come. One of my teachers had told me in a reading that I would be entering a quiet time.

She explained that these quiet times are when the Soul assimilates and integrates what has just been learned and then applies it in daily life. It is one way we can gauge our progress.

If we can apply what we have learned when a real-life situation occurs, then this prepares us for our next period of advancement. It is a balancing and recalibrating. Little did I know how much I would need to call on my learning in the next few years.

It is in these times of testing that all of the tools and techniques we have learned can be used to help us navigate the circumstances of life.

One such circumstance happened with the passing of my father. About a year before his passing, someone had told me in a reading to keep an eye on his health.

A few months later, I had a very prophetic, precognitive dream in which a helicopter with a skull and crossbones painted on the belly was hovering over my parents' house. I was very clear about the meaning. It was to prepare me for what was to come. A little more than a year later, my father transitioned to the spirit world.

My world, as I had known it, would never be the same. The incomprehensible had happened. I knew friends who had lost a parent, but how could this happen to me?

The larger question was, "How could it not happen to me?" After all, I was experiencing a part of the path that everyone must face sooner or later. It was still devastating. How could the world go on as if nothing had happened? I had to face the fact that my father was in the spirit world.

Less than two years later my mother joined him. Again, I had a precognitive dream that alerted me to what was to come.

I saw my mother and father sitting in the back seat of a car. They were both looking straight ahead. Their eyes had an otherworldly appearance. They were looking past this world into the next one.

Since my father was already in the spirit world, I knew that my mother would soon be joining him. She passed two weeks later. I knew that she was ready to go based on conversations I had had with her after my father passed.

Still, I was devastated when she passed because I was an orphan at age 41. I cried out to the Universe:

> *How could this happen to me? How am I supposed to handle this?*

They said:

> *We never give you more than you can handle. Draw upon what we have taught you. We will never desert you. We are always there for you. Call on us, and feel our comforting presence."*

So, I drew heavily on what I had learned about metaphysics to sustain me through that period. Although nothing could lessen the pain of not being able to physically touch my parents, the things I had learned helped me to keep moving.

One of these teachings centered around the death or passing of an individual. In the traditional religion of my childhood, the teaching was that, "We don't know when God will take someone," or "I don't know why God had to take him."

In my metaphysical studies I had learned that before we incarnate into a physical body, we sit down with our guides and teachers in the spirit world. All of the circumstances into which we will incarnate are decided upon, including the contract and life lessons we are to learn.

There are several exit points or times at which the physical vessel can experience death, and they are part of this discussion. The method as well as the timing of the passing also are part of this discussion.

When one of the potential exit points arrives in an individual's life, he or she may choose to leave, or he or she may choose to stay depending on others involved. This understanding cancelled out the notion of "I don't know why God took him."

I understood that this was one of the natural exit points in my father's contract, that all factors had lined up for this event, and that he had chosen to leave. The same concept applied with my mother. This understanding helped me immensely as I navigated through the many practical things that must be done after someone passes.

Just to make sure I had mastered the teaching, the Universe presented me with a similar scenario three years later when an uncle passed. Again, I had the familiar precognitive dream of seeing his eyes have an otherworldly appearance as if he were looking past this world into the next. Again, I was very grateful for the warning the Universe had given me.

After all that had occurred in that space of four years, I needed a time out. I was also going through a divorce around the time of my mother's passing, and I had been given administrative duties at work in addition to my teaching responsibilities.

I had entered a quiet time where I was incorporating all of the metaphysical teachings and focusing on earthly responsibilities. I also felt as if I didn't want to have any more precognitive dreams about death or hear any more bad news. I just needed a time out. And this is exactly what the Universe was giving me.

For several years I focused on earthly, day-to-day matters – paying bills and coping with a very heavy work schedule. I had not abandoned my metaphysical lessons – they were in the background sustaining me – but I needed that time to focus on the details of life and to rest. Just to rest.

Ready to Resume

Then one day the Universe decided to see if I was ready to move forward.

While I was looking at a yoga magazine, I noticed an advertisement for an event at a yoga retreat in the Bahamas. I remembered that my former yoga teacher had previously gone there and had enjoyed it. So, I signed up for the event and reserved a rustic beach hut right on the beach of the retreat location.

As soon as I arrived at the retreat, I knew that I had made a good decision. I could lie on my bed, look out at the green foliage, smell the fragrant blossoms, and listen to the waves lapping gently on the beach.

I thoroughly enjoyed my time at the retreat. The Hatha yoga classes, chanting, spiritual discussions, and simple food were just what I needed to ease back onto my spiritual path.

A humorous experience occurred during a yoga class under the palm trees. I was relaxing in the corpse pose when I heard the tourist tour boat returning to the town harbor. The tour boat was playing the song "Yellow Bird," a popular party song at that time. Hearing a party song during meditation time was quite a dichotomy. This reminded me that spirituality can be fun as well as serious.

At the end of the retreat, I felt refreshed and rejuvenated.

Although I didn't realize it at the time, this was a test for me because I had never traveled out of the country alone to go to an event where I knew no one.

I had successfully made all of my reservations and navigated immigration, customs, and foreign taxis all by myself. I had met people with whom to talk while I was at the retreat, and I had proved to myself that I could travel alone.

I had passed this test with flying colors! This would prove to be very helpful many years later when I began traveling on spiritual pilgrimages with like-minded individuals.

A few months later, I reconnected with a friend I had met ten years earlier who was teaching several spiritual classes including Reiki. I had come full circle back to my beginning. I knew it was time to resume my studies.

I entered into another time of intense study – re-taking Reiki I and continuing on with Reiki II and Advanced Reiki Techniques, meditation, dowsing, and many other energy modalities. I was finally in an environment where I could freely share with others of like mind.

No matter how much I had to keep my beliefs to myself during the workday, on the nights when I went to classes on spirituality and metaphysics, I could relax and be myself. I could let my voice be heard.

Another Passing

During this time of intense study, my significant other became ill and passed. Again, the Universe had warned me about this in a dream. I saw the familiar scene of the eyes looking from this world to the next.

I cried out to the Universe:

How can I handle another passing? This is too much!

My Guides responded:

Remember, dear one, we are here with you. We will help you through this.

I thought about what they said, and I realized they were right. Aren't they usually right? After all, they can see things from a higher perspective. So, I moved forward.

Although one is never prepared for someone to leave, I was glad I had been forewarned. It was another time of great adjustment, and again, I relied on my beliefs and my metaphysical friends to help me through this test.

In my quiet time, I received an image of a building made of a child's building blocks. Suddenly, the blocks were thrown into the air, and some of the pieces were removed. The original building could never be reconstructed because some of the pieces were missing. A new building would have to be made from the remaining blocks.

It was a good analogy of what occurs when someone passes. A new step on the path must be taken because it is not possible to return to the previous one. Conditions have changed.

It was during this time that I came across the quote from the ancient Greek philosopher, Heraclitus, who said, *"You cannot step into the same river twice, for the water into which you first stepped has flowed on."*

I knew that I had to keep moving and that my spiritual path would keep me going.

More Study

So I continued to study. Sometimes we take courses of study without knowing how we will use them, but we simply feel drawn to them.

Shortly after my significant other passed, the Universe placed before me two opportunities that tugged at my heart. They included a chance to take a hypnosis certification course and another to become ordained as a minister in a non-denominational church. These were two areas in which I had long been interested, and the Universe opened up these opportunities at a time when I was ready.

The hypnosis course gave me further insight into the workings of the mind, and it would be very helpful later as I developed personal meditations.

The non-denominational church offered me the freedom to express the varied aspects of all of the different religious paths I had explored. It also was refreshing to be with others in the group. I knew that with this group, I could continue to be free to grow and develop and express myself.

It was very synchronistic that my completion of the hypnosis class and my ordination both occurred in the same weekend. They were two more steps along my path.

I also continued participating with the study groups I had joined earlier and could feel myself being prepared for something new. It would come sooner than I had realized.

An Increase in Writing

As I continued with my studies, my writing became more prolific. I would awaken early in the morning and meditate before going to work. During these meditative times, I would often receive messages from my guides and teachers. The thoughts would appear in my mind as if a gentle process had placed them there.

Very often phrases and combinations of words were used that were not ones that I normally used. I began writing these messages in a journal, because if I did not record them, I would have no recollection of them later. I would come to learn that all of this is a sign that the messages are channeled from Beings in the Higher Realms.

One morning in early 2002, I received the following writing during my meditation:

> *The path is paved with beautiful stones. Each stone is a stepping-stone on your path. Enjoy each stone as you reach it, and be willing to release it and let it go in order to be ready to receive the next. This is what is happening with your job.*
>
> *Fully embrace the experience and let it go. This will happen with all of your experiences. Fully embrace them and let them go. Most people clutch and hang on so that there is no room for anything new to come in.*
>
> *When you release and let go, everything is fluid and flowing in a natural manner. You will naturally be attracted to where you need to be. Just let everything flow, and it will be there for you.*

This was to be a very prophetic writing for what was soon to come.

Insights from the Labyrinth Walk

About a month after I received this writing, I went for a walk on a labyrinth at a local church. I had always resonated to the thought of walking a labyrinth, but this was my first opportunity.

We were given a beautiful journal in which to record our thoughts after we had completed our walk. I was amazed at what I received:

> *Take time to pause at the turns in life to regain balance and direction.*
> *Be prepared for the unexpected. You will be guided.*
> *Persevere, for the course will change.*
> *Take time to enjoy the journey.*

Don't be so concerned about the path of others that you ignore your own.

Be serene, for life is sweet.

Don't let little things throw you off balance.

Don't be in such a rush. Slow down!

Remain sure-footed throughout the journey.

Don't look so far ahead that you forget the present.

When you seem lost, just keep following the path.

Free for New Adventure

Very soon all of these pieces began to fall into place.

Monetary resources and funding are a factor no matter where you are employed – public or private agency or self-employed. There are bountiful years, and there are scarce and lean ones.

In 2002 the agency where I was employed experienced a very lean year. It would be necessary for the agency to reduce personnel to balance the budget.

We were told that those of us who were close to retirement with the requisite age and length of service could possibly be eligible for an option where we would be given a severance package in exchange for having our position abolished.

This was an unexpected opportunity for me, since I had expected to work in that career for two more years. I had not even thought about what I might want to do after leaving that career. How would I spend my time?

Would I be bored? Who would I be without the identity of my position? Friends told me I would have more than enough to do and not to worry.

When the official offer came, I had two choices. I could stay for two more years, or I could retire. I had loved my career and worked with many wonderful people. However, I knew that the Universe was opening the door to the next stepping stone on my path. So, when the offer came, I checked "Yes" and sent the letter on its way.

One month later, my last official day of my 31-year career arrived. It was a bright, sunny summer day with a beautiful blue sky. My co-workers had arranged a surprise lunch for me even though my official retirement luncheon would be held on another day.

It was a surreal feeling to realize that this was my last day of that long-held career. When I walked out of the door at the end of the day, I had no title, no business card, no identification badge, and no job responsibilities.

I was now on my own. I was free and ready for the next adventure on my path.

Part 3

~~~

The Beginning
Of a New Chapter of Life

I adjusted to retirement very quickly. Almost before I knew it, many new opportunities came my way. They ranged from study and learning to writing and teaching.

Each of these areas allowed me to explore different aspects of myself. Each exploration of an aspect represented another stepping stone on the path. Each step led me to the next.

The Power of the Pen

As I had more unstructured time in my morning schedule, my writing increased. The freshness and renewed energy of the early morning hours proved to be very conducive to receiving information and guidance from the Universe.

Each morning I would pose a question such as "What do I need to know today?" Some days I would ask for more specific information.

One day I asked:

What do I need to do to raise my vibrational level?

I received a beautiful answer:

Pray, meditate; make all of your life a working prayer and meditation. This can be done by giving intentional focus and analysis to your everyday tasks. After you begin to practice this, it will become automatic and you will constantly be in communion with Me.

You can use whatever techniques and aids please you to have your surroundings reflect a meditative atmosphere. The feeling you need to achieve is peacefulness and joyfulness. These states are conducive to my helpers – the angels and guides – to work with you on an ongoing basis and for you to be able to hear them.

Another day I asked:

What do I need to know today?

I received:

Be careful with your feelings. Be careful with the feelings of others. Life is fragile. It is like a beautiful rose with dew on the petals. Just enough sun will help it to open, but too much will dry it out. You can regulate the amount of sun.

Be diligent in your studies, and we will reward you greatly. Apply yourself so that we can work with you. The more you study and apply what you have learned, the more we will be able to work with you. Life is not always easy, but it is on the growing path. Each day is an opportunity for growth and development. Set a good pace that you will enjoy.

When one focuses on higher things, the daily tribulations seem to disappear. As you focus on higher things each day, it will seem more natural, and you will look forward to it. It will feel like a time of rest, retreat, and renewal.

After I had received the answers to these questions, I realized that I only had to ask the question, and almost immediately an answer would be given by my guides. What a realization! It was like having my own personal advisors at the ready!

The Ascended Masters

I had long been interested in the Ascended Masters. Each time I saw or read a book about them, I felt a tugging at my heart, a wanting to know more about them and their teachings.

I had read that they were very advanced Beings and that they had transmitted wisdom teachings through various channels throughout the ages. I also knew that some of the Ascended Masters were associated with the different Rays of Light and that certain gemstones also were connected to each Ray.

I wondered about the connection of the Rays and how they applied to me. Then I received an answer.

First I asked:

How do the Rays of Light work?

They said:

The Light is composed of Rays. When you pass light through a prism, it will separate into different colors. Each color represents a Ray. Each Ray represents a different quality that is an integral part of the whole. Without each Ray of Light, the composite Light would not be the same.

It is the same with persons who resonate to the different Rays. Each person carries a certain quality. When persons come together to work on a task, each aspect is represented. One person may express love and compassion. Another may express a logical train of thought. When the two aspects are combined, a spectacular product emerges. The whole is greater than the sum of the parts.

Then I asked:

How do the gemstones relate to this?

They said:

Each jewel contains a wealth of knowledge. This is why people are attracted to jewels. They are attracted to the vast treasures of knowledge hidden within, but they do not realize this. They see only the outer beauty when it is really the inner beauty and knowledge they seek.

The jewels promise a richness. They hold the vast inner secrets that can only be unlocked by studying them. This is why each of us on the inner Rays has our own jewel that represents us. We are the guardians of that particular Ray of knowledge.

This is why at times you will resonate with one jewel, and at other times, you will resonate with another. Just as all colors make up the rainbow, all jewels are precious. There is no competition, for without one, the others could not exist.

So it is with the teachings. They are interdependent. This is what we had hoped you on the Earth plane would learn – that you are all interdependent. One race is no greater than another, nor one nationality, nor one religion, for you are all needed to make your Earth a place of harmony.

Keep picturing peace, for it is you – the Lightworkers – who must hold this vision if it is to succeed. As more and more Lightworkers realize their calling, the vision can increase.

When it reaches a critical mass, it will overcome the darkness that is now permeating your Earth. War is not the solution. The solution is holding the vision of peace. We need additional workers to hold the vision of peace.

This can and will succeed if enough of you spread your Light.

It cannot be mandated or coerced but must be done in love.

– Received from El Morya, Ascended Master of the First Ray

As I reflected on what I had received, I felt a special closeness with the Ascended Masters and wanted to know more on how I could communicate with them more effectively. I remembered the earlier writing about having a special place from which to receive their beautiful teachings.

I wondered:

How can I create my own special place?

They replied very promptly:

Your special, sacred place is an etheric crystal palace cave high up on the mountains above the fray down below. The crystal palace is oval shaped and also round. It is crystal and faceted, and the color can change depending on the vibration you need.

It is your place of safety, teachings, and healing. When it was first shown to you, it came in violet or lavender, for this teaching. Today, it is coming in the pink of pink topaz or rose quartz to impart the love vibration of Lady Nada.

Your teachers will change from time to time. The other day your teacher in the cave was Sananda, Jesus the Christ. Today, it is I, El Morya, and Lady Nada, who came to assist you with your class.

I asked:

This is all very fascinating, but how do I have a reminder of this in daily life?

They said:

Begin to build your collection of crystals. Have those of different colors and vibrations. Each one will be a reminder of the quality you are focusing on. Each one is precious. Treat each one as a treasure. They are a reminder of a higher vibration.

So, I began my collection of crystals. I had been collecting rocks since childhood. My favorites had been rose quartz, milky quartz, and granite. Now, I could see the connection between my early fascination with rocks and the higher implications of crystals.

A Preview of Things to Come

Soon after I began to receive the written messages, I decided to go for a reading with my teacher from whom I had taken channeling classes. She covered many areas included in my questions, and then she turned to the guides and teachers who were working with me.

She said that I would become acquainted with an angel who would be working with me. His initials were A-Za. He presented himself as male energy that was pure love, and he was radiating much light. He was accompanied by another angel who presented herself as a female with dainty pale skin, golden hair, and white wings.

It would be much later as my channeling began in earnest that I would go back and realize the importance of this information and how it would materialize.

Reconciling Religious Paths

As I continued to write and receive messages from my guides and teachers, my thoughts turned to how I could reconcile all of the various religious and spiritual concepts I had experienced.

My traditional upbringing in the Methodist church gave me a

Christian view of religion, and my early writings used terminology of that perspective. Yet I felt that I didn't have the complete picture of everything that existed.

When I began my metaphysical studies, I read *Autobiography of a Yogi,* by Paramahansa Yogananda. I resonated very strongly with the Hindu concepts, and I liked the straightforward approach in which they were presented.

As I mentioned earlier, a friend suggested a yoga teacher, and I began taking Hatha yoga classes. I especially enjoyed the chanting and yogic philosophy that she included.

Then I began attending another church in which natural law and messages from the spirit world through mediumship were emphasized. I resonated very strongly with the natural / universal laws, and I was fascinated with the mediumship and messages from the spirit world.

After the passing of my parents and going through my divorce, I decided to return to a more traditional path, and I attended an Episcopal church. I enjoyed the ritual and felt secure being part of a mainstream tradition.

Soon, I began to feel the urge to go back to the church that emphasized natural law and mediumship as well as to return to a yogic tradition. Why did everything have to be so separate? My heart yearned for parts of each path.

After much reading about religion and spirituality, I realized that there are many paths to the mountaintop.

Still, I wondered how I could reconcile all of these paths within myself.

So, I decided to meditate and contact my guides:

> *How do I reconcile my attraction to each path? Why do I have to choose? Do I really have to choose one path over*

another? Do I have to be on just one path? I want it all!

They heard my plea and responded quickly:

Before you were, I was. Before there was a division of religions, you were. You were part of me, as were all souls. Then you and all others were spun off. I am the One. This is why you are having such a hard time with selecting a man-made division of religion. In reality there is no division.

There is only One, and there is only The Law. The Law is from The One and governs all things. Man has created religion because he needs a figurehead and more literal rules than The Law.

The Law is pure and simple and cannot be divided. It was never meant to be divided. It was meant to remain pure and whole. When you teach from the higher level, you are teaching a purer form of The Law. This is the level to which all must return before they can return to Me. The Law is One. The One is All.

The Law of One has been my promise to you, My Children, since the beginning of time. The Law rises above ego, above time, above space, above all that is except for Me. Look to The Source, and you shall be free.

Jesus, the Christ, was one of my messengers, not the only messenger. He was a way-shower as was The Buddha and others. No one and no path has an exclusive handle on the path back to Me. It is open to all who desire it.

There are many paths to the top of the mountain. It is ordained that it should be so. Believe in The Truth, and The Truth shall set you free. All of you are my chosen children. – God

Wow! Was I ever relieved!

This answered my question about spirituality in its original form. I later learned that different spiritual messengers had come forth at different times during history. They brought the teachings in a form and terminology that the people of that time could understand.

Very often, after the passing of a teacher or prophet, his followers would form a religion around his teachings. As the teachings were handed down and translated, the original meaning and intent were sometimes changed. Often, the slightest change could alter the meaning and interpretation.

As this occurred, a struggle among the various religious paths developed with each group stating that its path was the only way to enlightenment.

It was no wonder that I felt so conflicted about choosing one path over another. I had aspects of each path within my Being. After all, the aspects had originated from the same Source.

So I decided to relax and enjoy the aspects from each path with which I resonated. I did not have to belong to a specific religion in order to be spiritual. At my core, I would always be a Spiritual Being.

Reiki Master Training

At the same time my writing increased, I also had opportunities for increased studies.

A good friend, who was a Reiki Master and from whom I had taken Reiki, decided to teach a year-long Reiki Master training, and I jumped at the opportunity. It felt very natural to be on this path, and because I had much unstructured time, I could focus on my studies and enjoy the process.

During the Reiki Master training, we were given the opportunity to learn what our predominant modality of energy work was. I learned that my strongest modality was distance work, in which I would tune in to the energy of the recipient and send energy. I found this to be very natural. It felt as if I had always known how to do this.

All I had to do was focus my energy with intent and send it to the recipient. I wondered why this seemed to be so natural, so I went into meditation and received my answer:

> *In this lifetime the ability to send the living light from the third eye has been re-awakened in you. Through your studies you have been reminded that this is a gift and that you are a channel. Because you learned this skill of sending energy during your time in Atlantis, you do not require extensive preparation for each sending.*
>
> *You know that you say a prayer, set your intent, and send the energy for the highest and best good of the recipient and all concerned. You give this freely with no expectation as to the outcome, for you understand that this truly is a contract between the recipient and the Universe.*

– Archangel Michael along with Metatron

Then I asked:

> *What is my responsibility to be certain that I am sending the highest and the best?*

They said:

> *Keep your own channel pure. Monitor your thoughts and emotions. Keep your own channel pure through no expectations of a particular outcome. Send energy from a perspective of love and know that you are sending the highest and the best.*
>
> *Set ego aside, for it is not about you and your ability. It is about your willingness to be a pure channel of love.*

I said a prayer of thanks for the re-awakening of this skill that had been lying dormant, waiting for the proper time to re-emerge.

More Ministerial Studies

During this time, I also decided to embark on a year-long study of learning more about the continuity of life, natural law, mediumship, and healing.

I had always felt an affinity for natural law, which some paths refer to as Universal Law. They had been among my earliest studies in metaphysics. Each time I studied them, I felt a resonance within my Soul.

I felt very much at home with these principles that transcended manmade laws. For me, they explained everything from an energetic point of view and provided guidelines for life.

I felt so drawn to them that I decided to become a minister at the church where I had taken this course of study. This involved another course of study, and I also faced the challenge of really letting my voice be heard in a more public way. I began giving lectures on natural law and spirit messages at the church with which I was affiliated.

My friends and my brother were very supportive of my new endeavors, and I could move ahead with gratitude for their support and encouragement.

Part 4

~~~

Am I on the Right Path?

As I continued my studies, I met many other people who were very accomplished in their areas of specialty. I felt doubts creeping into my thoughts. Would I ever be as advanced as they were? Did I really have what it takes to do this work? Am I on the right path?

I called out to my guides:

Am I on the right path? Can I do this?

They tried to calm my fears with an immediate response:

Do not compare yourself with others. You are where you need to be. Just be yourself. We can work with you easier this way. You have a unique path, as does each person. The outer trappings are just wrapping for the inner work. This is where the progress can be made. You are doing fine. All is well.

I decided that if I didn't continue with my studies, no matter how many doubts I had about my abilities, I would always wonder what I might have done if I had overcome my fears. So, I forged ahead.

I successfully completed my Reiki Master Training, which included teaching a class to the rest of the participants.

In the classes on natural law and mediumship, I learned to bring through messages from Spirit.

I had overcome my fears and moved ahead on that step of my path.

Teaching Spiritual Workshops

Soon after I completed the Reiki Master Training, my good friend and mentor who taught the Reiki Master Training, asked me to co-teach some classes on prayer.

Was I capable of doing this? I was very accustomed to presenting talks on a variety of life skills, but this was a new experience for me. I would be speaking on topics that were much more personal.

I checked with my guides, who said:

> *Beloved, it is time for you to spread wings. We have prepared you for this along with own extensive preparation.*

There was no more hiding what I believed. So I took a deep breath and forged ahead.

We taught several workshops, and I really liked co-teaching. I loved the back-and-forth flow between us, and I felt like I was in my element teaching metaphysical and spiritual topics. We had included a blend of traditional aspects as well as metaphysical ones, and it was a bridge for me between the traditional and the metaphysical. It felt like this was what I had prepared for during my previous thirty-one year career.

It was as if the Universe had placed me in my previous career to learn everything that is involved with the logistics of setting up workshops, planning what to teach, and then teaching. It is in the looking back that I can see that everything was in Divine Order.

More Metaphysical Studies

During the time I was taking classes on natural law and mediumship, I met someone who connected me with another metaphysical teacher. I was accepted into her class, and another new world began to open for me. We studied channeled writings, and this rekindled my desire to resume channeling. I began practicing and felt my heart sing.

One of the first Beings who came through in my channeling was El Morya, the Ascended Master of the First Ray. He spoke about the will of God and the new consciousness.

Then I received a message from Mother Mary who said:

> *Beloved, we have worked together many times over the aeons. I will be bringing you some writings, and I am also working with you to bring forth more of the Divine Feminine energy.*

I was excited about this because I felt very drawn to the Divine Feminine.

To further confirm my work with the Divine Feminine, Lady Nada came through with a brief message:

> *Dear One, We have worked together many times over the past few years. I am also here to assist you with the Divine Feminine energy.*

I was elated! Working with the Divine Feminine felt so good!

Meeting New Teachers and Mentors

While I was attending the metaphysical classes, my teacher introduced me to another teacher who was to become a very important teacher and mentor on my path. She, in turn, introduced me to another teacher and mentor at a seminar held a month later.

As I entered the conference room of the first seminar, the air was full of electricity. I had never felt such a high vibration at a workshop. I knew this was going to be very special.

As I listened to the discussion and participated in the meditations, something inside me shifted. I could feel my own vibration rise to a higher frequency. Once again, my heart began to sing.

What was I feeling? What was I supposed to know? Was this a signal?

I felt Archangel Michael come in:

> *Dear One, of course you are supposed to be here. This is your next step.*

It was as if the Universe had lined up each step for me. My role was taking each step as it was presented.

Discernment on the Path

People who have a need to please others very often try to be all things to all people. They may say "Yes" to requests when they really want to say "No." They may pursue activities because they think it is expected of them. When this happens, schedules can become overloaded very quickly.

After I had been retired for some time, this happened to me. There were many activities I wanted to pursue. I soon found that each day on my calendar had at least one activity and sometimes two or three.

I thought back to the time just before I had retired when I was wondering what I would do. Then I understood what others who were already retired meant when they said, "I'm so busy I don't know how I ever had time to work."

The truth for me was that I was trying to cram in everything I had always wanted to do but for which I had never had time before. Now that I had total responsibility for my schedule, I had put everything on it.

Recognizing this, I suddenly felt exhausted. I realized that I needed to exercise discernment and determine what was really most important to me.

I felt myself still being pulled between the expectations of the traditional path and the metaphysical path. Most people only knew me as someone who was on a traditional path, even though my heart was encouraging me to pursue a more metaphysical path.

I knew that the further I continued on my path, the more I would begin to publicly show what I was feeling in my heart. If I were to continue to honor myself, I could no longer be all things to all people. I needed to set boundaries.

As I wrestled with what to do, I received a writing from my guides and teachers:

> *Don't try to be all things to all people. When you do, you run yourself ragged. When you run yourself ragged, you become an automaton. You become a human doing instead of a human being. Would you take your best friend or closest family member and run them ragged? Of course not.*

> *When you talk about the Golden Rule and treating others as you would have them treat you and pair this with the commandment to love thy neighbor as thyself, how can you reconcile your actions? If you don't treat yourself well, you can't let your love flow outward. There is nothing to give because you have run the well dry by running yourself ragged.*

> *This is the same advice that is given on airplanes to put on*

your own oxygen mask first before assisting others with theirs. You can't give what you don't have. When you determine what is really important to you and focus your thoughts, feelings, and actions in this way, you are living a harmonious life because you are living in accordance with your core self. This leads to a simplified life.

When you go to a buffet table, do you eat everything in sight, or do you select what you really like? Do you come away from that meal satisfied, or do you come away miserable because you ate everything?

Life with all of its possible activities is like a buffet table. You are to select your favorites. Then you come to the end of the day knowing that you have done that which is really important to you. Do you say, 'I'll do that tomorrow,' or 'I'll do that when I'm older or when I get out of this or that?'

Take action now. The present is all there is. You never know how much time is promised to you. Spend each day in such a way that, when you are getting ready for bed, you can say, 'I really enjoyed this day. This was fun.'

Get in touch with your core values and priorities. Review them periodically. Make changes if something has changed in your priorities. They aren't set in concrete. They are yours, not someone else's.

Be true to yourself. In this way you can be genuine to others. You are on this Earth to live your path, not somebody else's. Do what you need to do for you, and others will benefit. They may balk at first, but hold your ground.

This is your life with your lessons. You are important. Treat yourself that way, and others will follow suit. Be at peace, for you have earned it.

I wondered why I had allowed myself to become mired in this situation of filling my calendar to the brim by signing up for every opportunity. After all, wasn't this what I had wanted? I was beginning to question what I had asked for.

I cried out to my guides:

What am I to do? How do I get out of this?

They responded promptly:

You are being presented with opportunities to set boundaries. These opportunities are there for you to define what is really important to you. Because there are no right or wrong answers, you are free to choose. Your answers, however, will define who you are and what you will be.

Small choices lead to big outcomes in any direction. There will be those who do not understand your path, no matter which one you choose. That is why it is important to make your choices and set your boundaries, for then you are in control.

I responded:

But you know I have trouble making decisions. How can I choose and know that I have made the right choice?

They quickly answered:

Choices always come in very tempting forms. It is no longer about choosing between one attractive and one unattractive option.

It is about choosing between two very attractive options. It is only when the options are analyzed and when the deciphering of what each option would represent, if selected, that the full impact of each option can be realized and recognized.

It is necessary for the two options to be attractive for the real choice to take place. It does not mean that one is better than another. It only signifies the rapidity with which one will progress.

Do not become involved in illusions, and do not pre-judge. You are on the starship ready to travel.

Whenever I receive the same message three times, I know this is a direct signal from the Universe to pay attention.

After receiving these writings from my guides, I realized that I needed to prioritize my desires, goals, and activities and focus my attention on what was most important to me as well as to take time to smell the roses.

My heart was really with my metaphysical studies. So I resigned my affiliation with the church where I had been lecturing. I also resigned from several other groups.

As I looked back, I was very grateful for what I had learned and the opportunities I had been given. Each group had provided me with exactly what I needed at the time and had provided the link to the next step. Now it was time to move forward yet again.

So I took a deep breath and stuck my foot a little deeper into the waters of metaphysical studies.

Part 5

~~~

A Shift in Direction

Soon after I made the decision to focus more on metaphysical studies, I attended an out-of-town, two-day seminar presented by one of my teachers and mentors, whose work I had been studying for several years and with which I resonated very deeply.

The day before the seminar began, I learned that my first channeling teacher and mentor from years earlier had passed. I was sad because I would miss talking to her in person, but I knew she would be watching over me as one of my spirit guides and teachers.

Then in the middle of the night between the two days of the seminar, I suddenly woke up and heard in my mind:

Do you wish to continue?

Without asking what continuing meant, I immediately said:

Yes.

I knew in the core of my Being that it meant moving forward on my path in a much deeper way. I could literally feel my direction shift at that moment. It was if I were looking at a clock set at 11:00 and suddenly the hands on the clock shifted to 1:00. It was a moment where I knew I had made a life-altering commitment.

This shift was confirmed a year later in a channeled writing:

You agreed long ago to bring the message of universality and not to be associated with any one religion. Your path is that of universality.

This is why you enjoy aspects of many religions but do not want to be confined by just one religion. When you agreed last year to let us shift your track and direction, this was the adjustment that was needed for you to be on your true path.

– Sananda

A further explanation soon followed:

The shift of path you experienced in April 2008 was the shift of your path from the third/fourth dimension to the fifth dimension. You knew at the time it was monumental.

*However, we could not tell you what it was, for it **was** monumental, and it would have scared you. We had to let you adjust little by little to changes in every area of your life.*

And change you have! It is reflected in your entire Being. This shift has permeated every cell of your body. Expect more changes, and be ready for them, for you are truly changing to a crystalline etheric Being.

Go with the flow, and all will be well. Keep your focus centered in the higher dimensions. All will be well.

– Lord Metatron, along with Lord Sananda, Lord Michael, Lord Melchizedek, and St. Germain

They also gave me some practical tips to maintain my sense of self in the Fifth Dimension and higher:

Remain in the moment.
Focus on your heart center, which also includes the high heart

center, just above the heart center.

Remain centered in the love you feel in your heart center.

Notice the lightness and the joy you feel when you are centered in your heart center. This is the love and joy of the higher dimensions.

Let go, gently and with love, of those things and situations that do not resonate with your higher state of vibration.

Be comfortable with your Light.

Teaching Metaphysical Classes

About a year later I had the opportunity to begin teaching metaphysical classes from the material I had learned from one of my teachers and mentors. I would be teaching alone, and this was a huge step for me. Fortunately, a friend offered to host the first series of classes, and I was on my way!

As soon as I began the opening moments of the workshop, I felt my guides and teachers come in, and they were with me all throughout the workshop. I realized that it was a partnership that included the host, the participants, my guides and teachers, and myself. Each person contributed to the energetic success of the workshop.

A new feature of this workshop was that I would be channeling a live message from one of my guides and teachers. I had begun doing some live channeling in one of the classes I had been taking, but this was the first time I would be bringing through channeled information in front of people I had just met.

This was really out of my comfort zone, and many doubts began to creep in. Would I be able to do a live channel in front of the group?

What if I opened my mouth to speak and no one came through? How long could I sit there and say nothing before panic would set in, or before the group would decide I didn't know what I was doing?

Even though I knew that other channelers had had these same doubts when they began, it was little comfort to me at that time. I was the one who would be expected to channel at the workshop.

The night before the workshop was to be held, I went into meditation and talked to my guides and teachers:

> *Dear Guides, You know this is a huge step for me to do a live channel in front of people I have never met. Please be there for me and come through at the time of the channeling. Better yet, please be there throughout the workshop. It begins at 10:00 am, and the channeling will be at 4:00 pm. I need your help! Thank you!*

They replied:

> *Dear One, Of course we will be there for you. Relax and let our energy flow through you.*

The sun dawned brightly the next morning. The participants arrived, and I was so happy to see them!

Just before the workshop began, I felt the energy of the Higher Beings come in. What a relief!

When it was time for the channeling, I told the group that we would see if anyone in the Higher Realms wanted to speak.

Of course, I knew they wanted to speak, but would I be able to bring through their message?

I centered myself, surrounded myself with white light, and said a silent prayer. Then, Archangel Zadkiel and Sananda (Yeshua) came through with brief messages! I was so relieved! I could feel their energy, and I said a prayer of thanks to them for their beautiful messages!

Later that night, I said another prayer of thanks, and they replied:

Dear One, We told you that we would be there. It is our pleasure to bring our messages and energy to share with the group.

A few weeks later, it was time for the next workshop.

I felt the same stress over knowing that I would be doing a live channeling.

The night before that workshop, I went into meditation and said to them:

Please help me! I don't know whether I can continue doing these live channels if I'm going to feel so stressed. Can you at least tell me the topic of the message to be channeled?

They replied:

Of course, Dear One, we will even give you the first two sentences to help prime the pump for the flow of our energy to come through. Stay relaxed and focused, and all will be well.

They proceeded to give me the topic and the first two sentences, so I had a restful night.

The next day, when the time arrived for the live channel, I followed their instructions. I said a prayer, relaxed, and focused my attention on them. I felt my conscious self step back, and they came in with a beautiful message that was tailored for the group.

That worked like a charm!

That night, as I was thanking them for being there and bringing the message, I asked:

That worked very well with knowing the topic and the first two sentences ahead of time. Do you think we could do this each time? I would feel much better with this arrangement.

They replied:

>*Dear One, Of course we will do that if it will make you more comfortable.*

They have been true to their word, and I am so thankful!

Channeling Increases

Meanwhile, my channeling increased. I was receiving messages from several Archangels and Ascended Masters – Archangel Michael, Archangel Zadkiel, Metatron, El Morya, Sananda, St. Germain, Serapis Bey, Lady Mary, and Lady Nada. Each one had a different energy and vibration, and I felt very close to each of them.

I knew from my studies that it would be easier if I chose one Higher Being to be the main one I channeled.

But I didn't want to choose! I loved all of them! How could I ever choose one over the others?

Archangel Michael replied:

>*Beloved One, Remember that in the Higher Realms, there is no competition. It is not a matter of choosing one of us over the others. We work together in our areas of specialty. We are all here to work with you at any time. We will all continue to love you.*

As I reflected on how they each came through during live channelings, I realized that Archangel Zadkiel came through the most strongly at that time.

This was not surprising since I had learned in a reading that I have a strong connection to the Seventh Ray of Light, of which Archangel

Zadkiel and Holy Lady Amethyst are the Archangels and St. Germain is an Ascended Master.

Then I remembered the earlier reading from one of my teachers who had said I would be working with an angel whose initials were A-Za.

I asked:

Archangel Zadkiel, is this you with the initials of A-Za?

He replied:

Of course, Dear One, let me give you a writing to introduce myself.

Beloved One,

Allow me to introduce myself. I AM Archangel Zadkiel, the keeper of the Violet Ray. This is the home of the Violet Flame, which is guarded by Beloved St. Germain.

Feel my energy, for it is my soul signature, and it is part of yours, also. Become acquainted with my vibration. I will visit you often, and you will be a messenger of my teachings. This is why your energy has been vibrating at a higher level for the past few days.

Keep your focus high. Reach for the stars, for they are your home. Know that you are greatly loved.

I AM Archangel Zadkiel.

So my course was set! I would channel Archangel Zadkiel as the primary Higher Being in my live channeling in the classes. Occasionally, another Being would come through to say hello. Often this occurred when someone in the class needed to hear from that particular Being.

At one class I had just finished channeling a message from

Archangel Zadkiel, and suddenly I felt another familiar energy:

I AM Metatron, and I have come to bring greetings.

He then proceeded to give a short message to the group.

After the class ended, one of the participants came up to me and told me that she was certain that Metatron came in because she needed to hear from him. She felt that the message was especially for her. I thanked her for this confirmation, and I said a special prayer of thanks to Metatron.

I noticed that a subtle shift was taking place in my channeled messages. Terms associated with certain religions were being replaced with universal ones.

Concepts of oneness and universality were the focus. The shift continued from the third dimension to multi-dimensional, from planetary to galactic and omniversal.

Developing a Website

As I continued to teach classes and channel, I realized that it was time for me to have a website. It would help spread the messages to a wider audience and reach people who could not travel to my seminars.

This was a huge step for me because I was still struggling to overcome the fear of speaking my truth. Having a website would be speaking my truth in a much more public way.

Then the next panic set in. Would I be able to channel an appropriate message each month? What if nothing came through? Would I be able to meet the expectations of my readers?

It was the same old panic of stepping outside my comfort zone. I was soon to realize that each time we step up to a new level, we have to confront our fears at that new level.

I needed to have a conversation with Archangel Zadkiel:

> *If I do a website, will you assist me by bringing through your beautiful messages?*

He replied:

> *Certainly, Dear One, it will be my pleasure.*

I said:

> *You know it will be every month and not just the occasional class.*

He replied:

> *Dear One, Time is not an issue with us on the other side. It is all relative because everything is happening in the present moment. A monthly message is perfect! It will give us an opportunity to commune on a regular schedule.*

So, I summoned the courage to move forward, and a friend agreed to be my webmaster. I felt very relieved when she agreed to take this on because she knew me and what I would like. I trusted her to develop a website that would reflect who I was and would do credit to the messages that I would be transmitting from Archangel Zadkiel.

I decided to name my website, Personal Pathways of Light (**www.PersonalPathwaysOfLight.com**), to reflect my belief that there are many paths to the mountaintop. Each person's path is a unique strand of Light in the beautiful tapestry of Light of the cosmos.

As I looked back at my own path, I could see that it began with a very traditional view of religion and had zigzagged back and forth between mainstream and metaphysical and arrived at a place of spirituality and metaphysics.

It is a path that will continue to evolve as I grow with additional life experiences. This is what makes life so exciting for me! Everything is fresh and new and always expanding!

Going Public

Finally, the time had arrived for my website to go public. My webmaster had produced a beautiful website that reflected who I was and what I wanted to share. Now there was no more hiding in the shadows.

Once the website went live, I would be sharing my voice and that of Archangel Zadkiel transmitting through me. Not only would I be sharing who I was, I would be very public with my channeling.

The night before the website was to go live, I took a deep breath. Was I ready for this? Was I ready to put myself out there?

Whether I felt ready or not, I had to move ahead. For many years, this was what I had prepared for. It was time to speak my truth in a public way.

The next morning my website was indeed live and public. I had launched myself on the next step of my path, and I was ready for more new adventures!

Soaring in the Dimensions

Bolivia

I was standing near the giant red rocks in the Valley of the Rocks, 13,000 feet above sea level in Bolivia. Suddenly I felt a very tall Being standing behind me. It was a Being of White Light between fifteen and twenty feet tall.

Its energy was warm and inviting and felt very familiar.

I had the impression that it was an interdimensional Hathor. I remembered the loving, gentle energy that the Hathors carry.

Then I had a realization. Had I worked with the Hathors previously?

It was as if the Hathor Being had read my thoughts and said yes, in an energetic way.

It said:

> *You have been with us on many journeys. This is just the beginning of what we have to show you.*

Egypt

I was standing in the small Hathor Temple at Philae in Egypt. I had just come from the larger Isis Temple. I ran my hands along the stone in the Holy of Holies. Something felt familiar. Had I done this before?

I entered the Hathor Temple of Dendera in Egypt. I looked at the giant, beautifully painted columns and ceiling. I went from chamber to chamber.

I felt the Goddess Hathor come in:

> *You were indeed here with us in Ancient Egypt, and we have much to share with you.*

I felt myself rise, and saw many adventures to come.

Epilogue

~~~

Lessons Learned Along the Path

I have learned many lessons along the path, and I still like to review them on days when I need a boost. These are some of my favorites.

Be true to yourself.

Don't give pieces of yourself away. If you do, soon you will not recognize who you are.

Real self-acceptance comes from the Divine Spark within, not from others.

Look within for guidance.

Live in the present moment.

Thoughts are energy. Therefore, energy can be regulated by thoughts.

Be honest with yourself about how you feel.

Listen to the signals from the Universe.

When you take one step, the next one will appear.

When you feel lost, return to the path.

Be bold, be brave, and move forward.

Be open to new possibilities!

Be true to yourself! Walk your own path!

About the Author

Linda Robinson is a spiritual writer and channel who brings messages from the Beings of Light. Her messages from Archangel Zadkiel and Lady Amethyst appear on her website. She is also a messenger for the Divine Feminine and the Hathors.

She has been a student of personal growth, spirituality, and metaphysics since 1978 and has taught workshops on these topics. In addition, she gives presentations at spiritual and metaphysical events.

Linda has a Master of Education Degree in Guidance and Counseling. In her previous career, she taught life skills to adults and youth in non-formal settings. She was also a volunteer on a crisis hotline.

A native of North Carolina, Linda has lived her adult life in the Hampton Roads area of Virginia, where she currently resides. She enjoys traveling and has gone on pilgrimages to sacred sites in Bolivia, England, Scotland, Egypt, Ireland, Greece, and the United States.

Visit Linda's website: www.PersonalPathwaysOfLight.com.